This book is dedicated to the possibilities…
in each of us and in all of us.

MY BOSS SUCKS

A STORY BOOK AND SURVIVAL GUIDE

BY BRYANT HALSTEAD AND ANNE BYRD

RIPTIDE PUBLISHING

Printed in the United States of America

Designed by Adam DeSio - DeSio Studios
www.desiostudios.com

Illustrated by Kelly Curtis

First Paperback Edition

ISBN 0-9778781-0-4

ACKNOWLEDGEMENTS

Adam Desio (www.desiostudios.com)
Adam is responsible for the layout, cover art, and the overall professional look of this book. He has helped us on numerous projects and is wonderful to work with…THANK YOU ADAM!

Kelly Curtis (www.kellycurtis.us)
Kelly is our illustrator, a former co-worker of Bryant's she experienced first hand some of the same bad bosses that he did. Kelly works full time as a Realtor with REMAX Super-Center in Virginia. THANK YOU KELLY!

Carolina Nickolic
Carolina assisted us with our initial editing when we first began the book. Her input early on was essential in getting us headed in the right direction. THANK YOU CAROLINA!

Vera Pastore
Vera did the final editing. She has years of experience and a keen eye along with a bar so high that it borders on perfection. THANK YOU VERA for taking this on and making us work hard through every revision.

Family & Friends
Thanks to all of you who have encouraged us and believed in us throughout this journey.

Former Bad Bosses
What can we say about you folks? Thanks for the inspiration. Yes, that's perfect. Without you this book would have neither been possible nor necessary.

We are truly blessed!

WHO WE ARE

Bryant Halstead and Anne Byrd are the founding partners of an extraordinary leadership development company called HALSTEAD.

Bryant is a former Marine with 14 years of progressive law enforcement experience, spanning line-level to command-level leadership positions. His professional leadership background enables a human-sensitive lens on leadership development in high-stress, high-change operating environments. (bryant@halstead.bz)

Anne's background is in operations and academia. She has 15 years of experience managing large call center companies, consulting organizations, and financial services operations. She has five years of teaching experience at the university level, and blends these skills into a dynamic training experience. (anne@halstead.bz)

WHAT WE DO

HALSTEAD'S leadership development training consists of unique experiential learning approaches. Participants leave HALSTEAD programs with different perspectives. We challenge customary beliefs around societal norms and awaken them to the possibilities that they have for themselves.

HALSTEAD offers a variety of training programs suited to the developmental needs of leaders and followers. Keynote addresses, half-day and full-day programs, and three-day and weeklong programs with established curricula can be customized to the specific needs of your organization. Our preference is to work closely with each individual client to create a customized program that specifically addresses your organization's needs.

HALSTEAD'S client list includes Fortune 100 companies, law enforcement agencies, and federal agencies. Our expertise is well suited to organizations that recognize how bottom line value is amplified through accelerated leadership development.

Program details, dates, references, and rates are available through us directly at:

HALSTEAD
P.O. Box 6153
Fredericksburg VA 22403
540-735-4944
www.halstead.bz

CONTENTS

ABOUT THIS BOOK

This book is about real-life situations with real-life bosses who suck. The stories are true (sadly), and while the names have been changed to protect "the innocent," the events and impacts are genuine. You will recognize the themes, and the gross absences of sound leadership judgment. You will hear the ring of familiar voices, the ache of opportunities cast asunder. These are stories from "your people," the kindred souls of those who have worked hard, been diligent, done the right things, and suffered the indignity of abominable leadership.

We created this book to help you learn about leadership. The stories are about experiences that we (Anne and Bryant) either had ourselves, or that were shared with us by friends, coworkers, etc. Each story concludes with survival tips – tools for you to use as you stare down your own boss-who-sucks challenge.

This book makes the point that while it really sucks to have a bad boss, there is something you can do about it. The stories give you those suggestions and they have been organized into two parts:

Part One – Bad to the Bone: stories about bad bosses.
Part Two – All About Me: lessons we've learned about ourselves.

ABOUT THIS BOOK

We both come from different leadership backgrounds. Bryant's experience is in the military and law enforcement. Anne's background is corporate America and academia. We've had different experiences and learned different lessons. You'll be able to "hear" who wrote each story through our different written "voices." We've included a final chapter that summarizes the survival tips and the primary author for each chapter.

Another point that we should mention is that many employees have had those perfectionist bosses who love to find mistakes in anything that people write. In consideration of those and any others who need it, we have strategically placed some grammatical errors, misspelled words, and other minor flaws throughout the book. If you're one of those people, go find them! If not, humor us and overlook them. Thanks.

We invite you to submit your stories online at **www.bossfixers.com** – about great bosses and bosses who suck. Also send us your thoughts about what this book revealed for you, and what we might do to make it better. We look forward to hearing from you, and hope you enjoy the journey.

ANNE'S THOUGHTS: MY BOSS IS AWESOME!

How often do you hear someone say, "My boss is awesome! She totally gets her role, my role, how to make the team work together, how to communicate, how to care about her people, and how to generate great results for the company! I love working for her, and I'd follow her wherever she went." We're guessing it's a small number. So if you don't know many people who have great bosses, and we don't know many people who have great bosses, where are the people who have the great bosses? Those bosses must be out there, right? Based on the statistics of successful corporations, they must be. How can we not know them? Where are they hiding? What are they doing?

We think the great bosses are the ones you never hear about. We think they are buried deep in organizations with a powerful network of people getting things done in ways that most companies don't know about and don't have systems to understand or duplicate. We think great bosses know their people, invest in developing their strengths, promote their growth and development, give great feedback, get things done efficiently and effectively, and go largely unnoticed by their organizational hierarchy. We think this because many corporations, despite their espoused values about people ("people are our most important asset"), don't know how to value great bosses. These great bosses are, after all, quite uncommon, a mystery almost, perhaps the unicorn of the business world, and in their virtual extinction unavailable for corporations to study, systematize, or duplicate. The great bosses are a threat to their peers (the ones who suck). They are rare, special, unique in his or her own way, and valued most highly by those who know them best and see them most clearly – their employees.

BRYANT'S THOUGHTS: THE POWER OF ONE

Wake up and smell the coffee. Why is it that as people climb the organizational ladder they end up becoming the boss that they hated or despised when they were at lower levels in the organization? Do they forget where they came from? Do they forget how they felt when people in those roles led them? Enough already! You didn't like it, and HELLO – the people that you're leading don't like it either. So STOP! It's that easy! All it takes is the conscious effort to be different, and it will be so. Change happens when one person sees the need to do things differently and has the desire and the tenacity to transform ideas into action. One person – that's all it takes. Are you that person? What would it take for you to be that person? 'Cause I've gotta tell ya, the world is full of people who will tell you what's wrong and what needs to be changed. You could fill stadiums with those people. What's rare is someone who sees the need for these changes and is willing to do something about it. Sometimes you can't even fill the seats on a motorcycle with those people. So which are you and which do you want to be?

What's this book going to do for you? Maybe the intent of this book is to open your mind to the possibility that your work environment can be different – if that's your desire. The old saying "that's the way we've always done it," and other similar phrases need to be history. We need to evaluate everything we do and why we do it, and change it when necessary.

BRYANT'S THOUGHTS

We value all the opportunities and experiences that were afforded us over the course of our careers. As leadership development experts and authors, we have found that personal experiences are a valuable teaching and learning tool, and trust that these stories will be seen in that light.

While on your quest of working for – or being – a great boss, change will be necessary. Nobody is perfect, and in sharing these stories, we do not intend to be disrespectful to the individuals. We merely wish to show you that transformation is possible. Transformation is the result of one person making a difference. You picked up this book so you are that person, and it only takes one. It only takes you.

INTRODUCTION
By Anne

Almost all of us have a boss and almost all of us wish we didn't. My son, at around the age of 6, shared with me in a spate of anger, "You are not the boss of me!" We, as human beings, struggle almost as much with the idea of having a boss as we do with the real thing.

Let's go back to the beginning. Most bosses, including us, didn't set out to be bosses. We didn't go to special boss school or boss camp. Most of us just "ended up" in the boss role, some of us by choice and others by the process of elimination. We may, as bosses, be the lesser of the evils or the best-in-class. Being a boss is a tough job, and chances are good that no one ever taught us how to do it.

If we go back to the beginning of your career, we will likely find that you didn't choose your boss either. Most of you just "ended up" working for the boss you're working for. You may have found that your boss is the lesser of the evils, or is the best-in-class. Your job – managing the relationship with your boss – is a tough job too. Chances are good that no one ever taught you how to do it.

Relationships with bosses are tricky because leadership is all about emotion. Most of us who are leadership trained were taught academic approaches that are rational.

INTRODUCTION

Unfortunately, leadership is not rational. Leadership is about the emotion created by you, your boss, and the situation in which you find yourselves. You are the only person who knows the emotional impact that your boss has on you. You are also the only person who can do anything about it. So what are you going to do about it?

If everything in leadership is specific to you, your boss, and your situation, why should you be reading this book? Because people learn from stories, and this book is chock-full of stories. Learning from a story means you won't need to learn as much through your own experiences. It's a shortcut, and a good one. We don't all need to beat our heads against a brick wall to know that it hurts. We can watch others and learn from them.

We did plenty of learning to get these stories! We didn't win in all of them, and you may not win in all of your learning stories either. We earned our lessons and we're sharing them to spare you the pain. We'd like to learn from your lessons as well, which is why we've invited you to share your bosses-who-suck stories with us for the next book. We think there's plenty of learning to go around, and we can't wait to hear from you. Enjoy the ride!

Part 1
BAD TO THE BONE

Bosses who suck (a.k.a. bad bosses) come in all shapes and sizes. There's no discrimination in the bad-boss category. Gender, age, or experience doesn't matter, and neither does title or rank. The size of a boss' paycheck doesn't matter. It doesn't matter what organization you work for, whether it's for profit or not, a government agency, an academic institution, or an all-volunteer organization. You can find a bad boss anywhere. And to make matters worse, someone who has been a great boss for others can be the worst boss for you, and the reverse is also true. You can never tell how you'll work with a boss until you are both in that situation. That sucks, too! Life would be much easier if you could take someone's "boss temperature" and determine whether he or she is normal or running a fever. Until someone makes that thermometer, though, you're on your own to figure out the whole good boss/bad boss thing.

Bosses, good and bad, require your attention. That thing between you and your boss – that is an actual, official, on-the-record relationship. There it is, the "R" word. In fact, it's most similar to the parent-child relationship with the boss being the parent and you being the child (in most cases). Isn't that great to know! The good news is that most of us know how to manage our parents, so we've got some experience that we can bring to managing our bosses. The bad news is that we probably don't like the idea that our bosses might see us or treat us like we're children.

Relationships, regardless of the flavor, require work. They require intentional communication, understanding, empathy, and courage. They require trust built through openness and honesty. Relationships also imply reciprocity, or tit-for-tat. That means expectations are involved. Expectations that go something like this, "I did something for you, now you need to do something for me." Because those expectations are usually implied, there's a lot of room for misunderstanding. Even when we are explicitly communicating there's plenty of room for misunderstanding. And trust us when we tell you that bosses, even good bosses, are not good mind readers. You actually need to tell them when you have expectations of them, and they need to tell you, too.

Yep – all this and all you do is work for the guy or gal. Relationships are big, complex deals, and if you have a boss or are a boss you're in at least one "professional" relationship. Remember when we said that leadership is about emotions? Relationships are what make that so.

Okay, so you are now officially managing a relationship with a boss that you think sucks. There's at least one thing (and quite probably many things) about this relationship that isn't working. In order to fix it, you've got some work to do. Here are the steps you'll need to follow:

1. Clearly identify the problem -- the part of the relationship that isn't working.

2. Determine and be able to articulate the different outcome that you'd like to create -- the change that you would like to see in the relationship.

3. Establish the actions that you and your boss might collectively take to produce this new outcome.

4. Execute your decision, and preferably in a way that lets you test your hypothesis and tweak it or stop it altogether if it isn't creating the expected outcome.

Hmmmm... What might be missing from that checklist? Perhaps the part where you actually communicate the problem to your boss? Yes, that would be the sticky wicket. That would be the part where many a brilliant fix-it plan comes undone. In order to actually fix the problem, you need to communicate to your boss that there is one. You need to find a graceful, tactful, won't-get-you-fired kind of way to tell your boss that things are not exactly perfect. We call it "feedback."

A myriad of sources offer great insight on how to give and receive feedback. You need to know that feedback is a skill. It takes practice to give and receive it well. We suspect that you already know how you like to receive feedback (and that the answer "I don't want any feedback" is not the answer.) Feedback is something you should be requesting routinely from your boss. Describe to your boss how you'd like to receive feedback. Ask him or her to do the same for you. This conversation opens the door for other conversations, and you will find yourself on the path to building a better relationship.

The stories that follow are about bad-boss situations, or troubled professional relationships. The tactics chosen to address those situations are just that – the tactics chosen to address those situations. They are not tactics that we recommend to you to solve your situation. You actually need to establish those yourself. Some of our tactics succeeded and some didn't. We leave it to you to decide.

CHAPTER 1

I'M RUBBER AND YOU'RE GLUE

A Bryant Story

Human beings, who are almost unique in having the ability to learn from the experience of others, are also remarkable for their apparent disinclination to do so.

- Douglas Adams

Remember this childhood taunt? "I'm rubber and you're glue. Whatever you say bounces off me and sticks to you." Feedback sometimes works like that taunt from our collective youth. Here's the story.

Ever have one of those bosses that had all the answers and got offended when you "pushed back" and told them something that they didn't want to hear? Many of these types of people are not good at receiving feedback either because they already have all of the answers or because they are not that interested in what you have to say.

I had a boss once that was just this way. Ideas were great if they were his and if not, they sucked, but wait… you might hear your idea again from him the next week when all of a sudden he had an awesome idea. Sound familiar? This same boss did not like to hear any feedback and was not at all adept at receiving it. He also wasn't so good at providing feedback to his people.

I had the opportunity to provide some feedback to him one day and I decided I'd seize the opportunity. This particular situation was one where he had asked me to take a look at operations in a certain section, between departments, and across the organization as a whole. It took me about two months to make the observations necessary to render an accurate assessment of the situation with suggested next steps. Once I completed this assessment we scheduled a meeting. On the day we met to discuss my observations he was very receptive and thanked me for my efforts. He wanted an opportunity to further process the information that I had presented to him and would get back with me on his decision and desired course of action. Looking back at this now, I should have asked for a more definitive timeline for his decision. What happened in reality was he just left me hanging for three weeks without even an update on where we were in the process. I had given him some valuable information about some strategic opportunities within his organization and his sense of urgency seemed to be non-existent.

By this point I had become very frustrated. Finally after being angered by his lack of response, I decided to ask for a status. He advised that he had reached a decision and we scheduled a meeting within the next couple of days. At our second meeting, he again stated that he appreciated my efforts and recommendations. However, implementing the recommended changes was not feasible at this time. I thanked him for finally rendering a decision and then he asked if I had any additional questions or comments. I thought now would be a great time to voice my opinion on the "waiting game" that he seemed to enjoy playing. Up until this point he had been very jovial because he was in control of the situation. As I began to relate to him how disrespectful it was to make people wait so long to hear back from him, his mood changed right before my eyes. He was having a serious "bio reaction" to the feedback that I was giving him, and man, was it powerful to watch. He knew he had to listen to what I was saying and apparently he agreed with me because he offered no reason whatsoever for why he had taken so long and still never got back with me.

That was a powerful learning moment for me. Never again will I miss an opportunity to provide feedback to someone that really needs it! Deep down it probably did him some good and it definitely made me feel a lot better! It also taught the importance of feedback and why I value it so much. It was clear to me at that point that my boss did not have much experience with receiving feedback. This should have been obvious to me due to his inability to offer any to anyone ever. With him it was a guessing game as to whether you were performing at or near the level he wanted. What's sad to me is the opportunity he missed and continues to miss for self-improvement and improving others.

So let's talk a little more about feedback and its value in developing people and the performance of organizations. First of all, the environment has to be set up for the safe exchange of feedback. People need to feel that they can offer feedback without the fear of repercussion. The creation and maintenance of this environment, in my opinion, is the responsibility of the leader or boss. This individual needs to walk this talk and set the stage for this safe exchange. The first step is to declare that feedback is a positive thing. It's all about mindset and practice. If you think negative things when you hear the word feedback, feedback will always be a negative for you. Reframe your thinking so that feedback is a positive thing.

Recognize that you will only get better with feedback, both positive and negative. Ask your boss for both, and provide him or her with both as well. Practice both and realize that your boss will be practicing, too. It may not be a perfect process, so give yourselves some space to learn and grow.

Feedback is helpful, positive, and essential to the success of relationships in both your personal and professional life. How else are you going to know how you're doing and how you're being perceived? You may be doing things that are incredibly annoying to others or ineffective and be totally oblivious to it. If given the choice of knowing versus not knowing, wouldn't you want to hear how you could improve?

SURVIVAL TIP

Be courageous and offer feedback to your boss. They'll never get better at receiving it if you don't teach them and maybe they'll appreciate your candor. If you have information that can help someone improve, it's your obligation to share it. Also, remember to ask for feedback if you're not getting it. It's valuable. Feedback is positive!

CHAPTER 2

DANCING BEARS

An Anne Story

Leadership exists when people are no longer victims of circumstances but participate in creating new circumstances.

- Peter Senge

MY BOSS SUCKS

What is up with those bosses who are so busy sucking up to their bosses that they can't or won't be involved with the real work at hand? We call those bosses Dancing Bears. They dance on their boss' command, be it to balance a ball or wear a funny hat. They build great upward relationships, sometimes roadblock their subordinates from upward access, and are generally most concerned with how they look from the perspective of senior leadership. Bears, in our opinion, should not wear tutus or funny hats, and they should not dance. Neither should bosses!

Dancing Bear bosses can be pretty to look at, and really unpleasant to work for. They can also teach us a lot. They do, after all, learn tricks that please their audiences and their trainers. According to the Gallup organization, the most significant influence over an employee's productivity is their relationship with their boss. If you get along well with your boss, you are more likely to be successful. Similarly, if your boss gets along well with his or her boss, your boss is more likely to be successful. The question then is what will they be successful doing? Will it be dancing in a funny hat or accomplishing the work that needs to get done?

Succeeding with a Dancing Bear boss requires that you shift your perspective. This boss could have organizational influence that could benefit you. He or she could be in a position to align resources like people, technology, and money around projects and causes you care about. Just like you, bosses care about things for reasons that make sense to them. You won't always have all of the same information or insight that your boss has, so you need to leave room for the possibility that he or she is making good choices for good reasons.

We need to introduce the topic of office politics here. Politics are a very real thing. They exist at every level of every organization, and you need to know that and learn how to operate within that reality. Managing your political well-being should be consistent with managing your corporate integrity. You want to be known for being great at what you're great at. You also want to be known for understanding how the organization works and being able to get things done within that construct. Should or could you also be changing the organization to your view of what would be a better place? Absolutely. And that's where your Dancing Bear boss can help. There should be room on your plate for both sets of concerns – those that would serve you well politically and those that would serve your own integrity.

The question you can ask yourself is what would it take for you to become part of the influence process, and create opportunities to advance concerns that matter to you? Start with a conversation with your boss. Ask him or her what it would take to elevate the priority of the projects or issues that you see as important and urgent. The answer should be telling. Listen inside the answer for what your boss isn't saying. See what you can learn about his or her perspectives and concerns. Your boss will tell you in the answer what he or she cares about. Start to align your priorities with what your boss cares about and watch the engagement start to shift.

Does all of this sound like sucking up??? Maybe. Does it sound like office politics??? Absolutely! Good employees get the game. They pay attention to how they show up, to who has influence and who doesn't, to how they can use the situation they're in to move things forward that they care about. What if we changed the name and called it strategy? Go ahead and change the name because that's what it is – the strategy of getting things done. How do you get what you need to get the job done? Sometimes that takes knowing who is pulling what strings and how you can become part of the show. The more upward influence you have the more things you can get done. Your Dancing Bear boss could be one of your greatest assets, so get yourself an interesting hat and your favorite clap-along tune. It's show time!

SURVIVAL TIP

Dancing Bear bosses are among the easiest to manage. They're predictable. They're pleasers. They get the lay of the upward political land. Use them to your advantage. Increase your ability to get your job done by aligning your strategy with theirs. Everyone will win.

CHAPTER 3

KING OF THE MOUNTAIN

A Bryant Story

Nearly all men can stand adversity, but if you want to test a man's character, give him power.

- Abraham Lincoln

MY BOSS SUCKS

Ever have a boss that reminds you of the phrase "King of the Mountain" or "Queen" if appropriate? Me, too. I'd like to share a story that was told to me recently about how conflicting corporate values - what the company said they cared about versus what they really cared about - made a man choose between his career and his family.

This is a Sheriff's Office story. The boss in the story held the rank of lieutenant. He had been promoted recently and with the typical zeal of a newly promoted supervisor, he was seeking to make a difference and establish himself in his role.

A mandatory supervisors meeting had been scheduled. This meeting was the venue during which our lieutenant-boss was planning to deliver some training on leadership to his junior-level supervisors. One of the first sergeants, a junior-level supervisor assigned to our lieutenants' division, had a conflict on the date chosen for the mandatory meeting. The meeting was to be held on a day that he was not scheduled to work, and he had a family commitment for which tickets to an event had already been purchased. When he brought up the conflict to the lieutenant he was told that this was a "mandatory" meeting and his attendance was required, NO EXCEPTIONS. Even when told about the fact that the tickets for this event were purchased well in advance of the date the meeting had been announced, the lieutenant held fast to his decision.

I must point out that this lieutenant has always preached the importance of family and this is supposed to be a "family focused" Sheriff's Office. Well, maybe not.

Confused by the position taken by our lieutenant-boss, the first sergeant went to another lieutenant and was met with the same response…BE THERE!   Feeling that he had no other option, the first sergeant went to the "mandatory" meeting with a plan to leave early so that he could still make his family commitment. Well into the meeting and on a break, the first sergeant asked how much longer the meeting would last. He was told that it would be over when it was over and that he needed to choose between his job and "going to play with his family."   Our first sergeant was stunned that someone in a leadership role in this so-called family-friendly environment would even think of saying something like that, so he went to speak with our lieutenant-boss' supervisor, the captain in charge of field operations. Sad news – same answer. The first sergeant resigned on the spot.

Wow, what are these people thinking? Who puts an employee in a position like that? Who says they run an organization under one set of rules and actually operate it under another? The answer – a lot of people, and therefore a lot of companies.

So what's the point of this story? There is a lot to be learned and understood about leadership and values. The story of this Sheriff's Office and its blundering leader-ship paints a great picture of what a values conflict looks like up close and personal. When an organization doesn't hold itself accountable for doing what it says it will do, its leaders have no "bright lines," or clearly defined boundaries, within which to operate. That puts the leaders – the people in positions of power – in the role of deciding what's right and wrong, accepted and not accepted, in any given situation.

The choices made by the two lieutenants and the captain evidence that they would be hard pressed to get anyone to follow them absent their positions of authority, as indicated by their titles, the shiny "brass" on their collars, and their starched white shirts. The organization set them up to make values decisions, and while they were at least consistent with one another, they were inconsistent with expectations that had been created by the organization for its employees. So hail the mighty kings. They allowed a talented asset to walk out their door over what boils down to an issue of ego: because I'm your boss and I said so. How many of those bosses can your organization afford?

One could argue that the leaders in this story actually wanted the first sergeant to resign – that they might have been inflexible on purpose. It's possible that they just aren't all that when it comes to managing performance, that they may just choose to make it hard for people to stay. That's one approach. It wouldn't be our preferred approach. But then this is a book about bosses who suck, and these bosses certainly do that!

We're sorry you gave up your job at the sheriff's office, dude, and trust us, you'll be better off for it!

SURVIVAL TIP

What leaders DO, what companies DO, is way more important than what they say. Listen to the talk they walk.

4
CHAPTER

A DOSE OF REALITY
A Bryant Story

I find it easy to portray a businessman. Being bland, rather cruel and incompetent comes naturally to me.

- John Cleese

Doctor, doctor, give me the news. I've got a bad case of running this place into the ground.

I've heard it said that the way Navy doctors cure a particular medical condition common to young Marines is to lay him on his stomach and give him a shot of penicillin in each cheek. Apparently it's such a large dose of penicillin that they feel the need to monitor his vital signs while they're giving it to him. The good news is that the doctors know how to cure the disease – they're not giving the young Marine two aspirin and telling him to call them in the morning. How many of our business problems "get solved" with two aspirin when what they really need is a healthy dose of penicillin?

The example that comes to mind for me is the Sheriff's Office for which I used to work and how they deal with manpower issues. The basic problem is that they need more people than they have. Rather than paint a compelling picture of their hiring needs, they lobby the Board of Supervisors to increase their overtime budget to a ridiculous amount. At my last association, our small Sheriff's Office spent more than half a million dollars in overtime expense. And be clear; the overtime is insufficient to cover the demand, so the department's leadership has spent the money, worked their people into the ground, and not solved the problem. They've given the department two aspirin and told their people (and the community they support) to call them in the morning.

A DOSE OF REALITY

Here's the order-of-magnitude math: at $50,000 per year (the average spend for a first-year deputy), the Sheriff's Office could have hired ten more deputies in lieu of the overtime expense. But even ten additional people (a whole squad) really won't solve the problem; the department probably needs about 30 people to totally solve their problem, or three years of overtime budget at their current rate of spend. At some point the Sheriff's Office should actually want to catch up against the staffing demand, rather than trying to play catch-up with overtime dollars. The leadership within the office has shown neither the willingness nor the ability to paint a compelling enough picture, or come up with a compelling enough argument, to support the demand for the additional people; thus two aspirin.

The dose of penicillin would be figuring out how many people they actually need to get the job done, thereby significantly decreasing the overtime budget or eliminating it altogether. The number of people the Sheriff's Office needs is determined by the size of the population and that particular populations' demand – their annual calls for service. Within that, statistics drive predicted growth in the population and how that growth will increase calls for service. There are national standards for ideal officer to citizen ratios, and the ideal number of average calls per officer per year. While the exact numbers don't matter for the purposes of our discussion, the point is that the calculation is easy to do. It's out there on a national level, and the leadership of the office has either chosen not to do the right thing or doesn't know how to do the right thing. Two aspirin.

This is a values conversation. Clearly the leadership of the office is concerned with getting the job done. What they're not concerned with is who they run into the ground in the process, or the impact that could have on their community. Are they bad doctors or do they just not care about the life and well-being of their patients?

Most business problems can get solved – even with the complexities associated with local politics and taxpayer dollars. Business leaders can understand and cure the root cause of the problem – the actual disease that is causing organizational illness – even when it's local or national government. Problems can get solved if leaders are smart enough, if they want a solution badly enough, if they're willing to care more about solutions than their own political careers, and if voters are willing to hold them accountable for a cure. Please give us the penicillin, monitor our vital signs while you do it, and give us what we need to get better… before it kills us.

SURVIVAL TIP

Hold your leaders accountable, help them improve by giving them your honest feedback, and have the moral courage to call out their inadequacies.

5
CHAPTER

THE KING OF DENIAL

A Bryant Story

The greatest discovery of my generation is that a human being can alter his life by altering his attitudes of mind.

- William James

MY BOSS SUCKS

Denial, Delusion, and Destruction… Some people seem so oblivious to the reality of what's going on around them. Do they really know and are afraid to do anything about it? Or, are they just clueless or self-destructive? The answers to these questions depend upon a lot of factors.

This story involves a former co-worker of mine who was completely burned out and ineffective in his assigned position. Rather than take control of his situation and actively seek out a cure for his woes, he just began to coast and do only what was absolutely necessary to get by. He spent most of his days socializing or surfing the Internet or engaging in any other activity that took him away from his responsibilities. He was suffering, his employees were suffering, and anyone that relied on the service that his organization provided was suffering, too, even if they didn't know it.

Fortunately for all concerned, he has been transferred to another position and this change of scenery seems to have given him a new outlook. He actually seems to enjoy what he's doing and it shows. Unfortunately for the people he left behind, his replacement and the others that received promotions due to his transfer may actually be worse than he was. It's one of those "better the devil you know" kind of situations, and that's another story entirely.

My point in sharing this story is to specifically call out that you are responsible for you! If things are not going well for you and it has a negative impact on you and the people around you, then do something to fix it! STEP UP. Don't be a boss that sucks and allow your employees to suffer for something you can control. You owe it to yourself, those who care about you, and anyone that's being affected by your current state of being. Have the courage to ask for help if you need it.

Another example of denial involves an individual who is apparently clueless regarding the state of affairs in the agency for which he is responsible. There are so many unhappy and even disgruntled people working for him it's disturbing. Why does he not know this? Or worse yet…does he know and not care enough to do anything to make it better? Either way, he has a responsibility to those people and the community his people serve. Now, the problem is that this situation is not noticeable from the outside looking in. It's much like a man who feels completely fine and goes to the doctor for an annual checkup only to discover that he has a terminal illness and only a short time to live. At some point, the poor health of this organization will become apparent to all, and there will be no cure to save those who should have been taking better care of it. At that point, someone new will come in and fix all of the issues that were previously ignored or neglected. The sad part of this is the impact on all of the people caught in the mix, those who don't have the ability to influence change, and those who are ignored or viewed as radicals for driving awareness.

There are a lot of bad bosses out there and most of them are not bad people, they're just in denial and are not all that effective in the leadership space. I don't have any sympathy for them because they have the information available that can help them improve. The key to success in leadership is to get people to want to follow you. If they do what they must for you only because of the position or title you have, that's not leadership, that's pathetic. Build relationships with these people, learn what's important to them, let them know you care about them, and take care of them. If you do this, they'll take care of you!

Sounds simple enough, right? Why, then, is it such an extraordinary event to find a leader who actually does it? The key to a leader's success is to pay attention to what works, what doesn't, and fill your leadership toolbox with the stuff that works. We all know what we want to see in leaders and what we don't. Remember those things so that in the future when you are assigned to a position of authority you don't become one of those bosses that you complained about.

SURVIVAL TIP

There's a ton of material available to improve your leadership ability. Take charge, step up, and go after it. If your boss needs help in this area and won't seek it out, maybe a few anonymous educational gifts should be considered.

44

6
CHAPTER

THE EYE OF THE BEHOLDER

An Anne Story

There is an enormous number of managers who have retired on the job.

- Peter F. Drucker

Remember that saying, "Beauty is in the eye of the beholder?" The same is frequently true for bosses. Bosses who suck get to keep their jobs because someone, perhaps even many people, think they are effective. This is the age of multi-rater feedback – you know, those 360-degree evaluation processes where your boss, your subordinates, and your peers get to provide feedback for your appraisal. These multi-rater or 360-degree feedback instruments have been translated into 16 different languages. They represent a $200-million dollar industry and have been used to provide feedback to over five million managers. How is it that more than five million managers know what people think of them, have had the opportunity to grow, learn, and develop, and yet we still have a world full of bosses who suck? The answer must be that we don't all agree on how bosses should lead or how they should make us feel.

There is an absolute ton of material out there on leadership and on being a good boss. There are taxonomies, tables, how-to guides, and how-not-to guides. There are dummy books and books for smarter people. There is research that contradicts the findings of other research, and there you are – working for the boss you're working for, wishing for a different outcome. Here's the thing . . . your boss can be exactly what you make him. You can take the weaknesses of your boss and turn them into strengths for you.

Two of my former bosses fit into this category. The first was a bull-in-the-china-shop type of manager. Why? People couldn't stand working with him. He singled out the wrong concerns and issues, and suggested that people had screwed things up when they really hadn't. I led about 150 people who processed loan applications. He was the Director who managed me and one other person who was responsible for the call center. I made sure I worked well with him and that the people around us loved working with me. I became the avenue around my boss, and through which people could get things done. My boss thought I was a total rock star, and the people around him gave him great feedback on me. I got three promotions in five years, and I worked for him the whole time. He, on the other hand, did not receive any promotions during that period. We both left the company and a few years later he called and asked if he could come work for me. I hired him. After all, I knew exactly how he needed to be led.

My second make-the-best-of-it-boss was a brilliant man, a brilliant analyst, but a really poor people-person. He was intimidating. He never made time for people. He canceled development meetings (if you could get them on his calendar). He didn't know how to give feedback – good or bad. He didn't even know what behaviors to look for to turn into feedback. But he was smart and I like smart, so I gave him a shot.

It turns out that he knew he didn't know how to do it, so he was afraid of it. He canceled development meetings because he didn't know what to say in them. He didn't know how to give feedback because he had never been taught. I took it upon myself to teach him. I enlisted the aid of some of my peers (reasonably good people-people), and we went about teaching our boss how to do it. We asked for feedback when we came out of meetings. We told him it was part of his job to pay attention to what we did and how we did it and then tell us what he thought about it as soon as it happened. We gave him space to learn, to be awkward, to make mistakes, and to fail some. In the process, we gave him space to improve. We developed a relationship based on mutual trust, and he turned into one of my favorite bosses ever. He's still not the best people-person – but he gets full credit from me for trying!

There's a special note here, and it matters a lot! If your boss has self-esteem issues, if he or she is threatened by you in any way, you are in one of the few (in my opinion) relationship situations that are impossible to improve. In fact, if this is the case, the counsel I would give you is to leave the situation. Helping a bad boss work through their stuff when they see you as a threat is a lose/lose situation. Trust me on this – walk away – no – RUN away – as fast as you can and as far as you can. There's just not enough that you can do to make that situation work out – for either of you.

SURVIVAL TIP

Identify your boss' weaknesses and play smarter. Take on the mindset that the whole is greater than the sum of its parts. Realize that your boss has weaknesses, set yourself up to compliment those weaknesses, and set yourselves up to be a stronger team.

7
CHAPTER

TICK TOCK
A Bryant Story

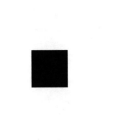

If I had to sum up in a word what makes a good manager, I'd say decisiveness. You can use the fanciest computers to gather the numbers, but in the end you have to set a timetable and act.

- Lee Iacocca

What's better than waiting? I don't know about you but patience is not one of my strong suits. If I want it, I want it now. If I need to know about it, I need to know about it now. I don't want to wait. I would daresay that most people, when they learn that something in the workplace will impact them, don't want to wait either.

Let's imagine you have a fabulous opportunity. A promotional opportunity has opened up and you believe that you're qualified for the role. It will change your life and your family's life. You post for the job. The posting deadline passes and in your mind the clock starts ticking. When are you going to hear? What are the next steps? What will the process be? Will you be selected to participate in that process? What should you do next? Tick tock. Tick tock.

Businesses create a cruel disservice to their current employees and their potential employees when they get them tremendously excited about the new opportunity and then fail to act quickly to fill the vacancy. The up-front process is bad enough, considering the posting, readying your resume, posting, testing, and anything else that may be required. Once you've been selected as a candidate, you interview for the job, and sometimes you interview with a number of different people. And then you're waiting again. When is the decision coming?

Shouldn't it be a high priority in business to move efficiently through the decision-making process and let people know the outcome as soon as possible? Applicants' lives could be revolving around this decision. They're excited about the possibility, they're afraid of the possibility. They need to know. We all need to know. So why take so long? Is it the intent of the organization to torture? In some ways that's what it is – mental torture. Are organizations so concerned about the accuracy, thoroughness, or validity of their processes that they need to check them end-to-end every time they are executed? Is that where all the time goes; or can managers just not decide? Are the options so good, so bad, or so hard to differentiate from each other that the managers just can't make a choice? What is it that takes so long?

Indecision, delay, or just flat out procrastination has a negative impact on the enterprise and serves no purpose. Every day people don't know who has been selected to fill the new role is a day that those candidates are not performing at 100%. Waiting becomes a drain on the brain, and unfortunately, excitement leaks out.

SURVIVAL TIP

Make a decision already! Do we need to put a gun to your head? What will it take for you to make up your mind and let your people off the hook? Please remember what it was like for you to be in that position. Instead of being a boss that sucks, if there's something you can do to make the process faster, more efficient, easier for your people and your company, please do it **TODAY.**

8
CHAPTER

KNOW WHEN TO FOLD 'EM
An Anne Story

It's easy to make a buck. It's a lot tougher to make a difference.

- Tom Brokaw

Texas hold 'em and you're dealt a deuce and a nine off-suited. Are you betting? The first turn does nothing for your hand. Are you still betting? If you are, let's play some cards and trust me, I'll have a bunch of your money! There are some hands you can't win with and you need to know when to throw in the cards. You lose your ante – that's it. Even if you have confidently bet on the come and it didn't come, throw in before you're sunk. There's not much bluffing in business; odds are you can't fake it long enough to wait out the other players. It's up to you to know when to toss in your hand, hold on to your stake, and hold out for a better play.

There are a lot of things you can do to help your boss improve, like offer feedback, to help your situation improve, to help your life not suck so much at work. This book is full of those examples. And then there are the situations you just can't win – when you're dealt a deuce and a nine off-suited. At work these "cards" are situations that are in total conflict with your personal values, or where your safety, sanity, physical health, or mental health are at stake. Here are a few professional "bad hands" that you should fold.

Bad Hand #1 - They're waiting for the next administration – LITERALLY!
This is a sad-but-true story. I was consulting for a federal agency and they were holding out – not making any changes – waiting for the next Republican administration. This was five years into the Clinton administration. Who knew when – or

if there would be a "next Republican administration?" Fortunately for that particular agency (I hope), the Bush regime has them at least taking SOME action – even if it's wrong. So if you're around a crew of folks who are waiting for Noah's Ark to pass by before getting on with the business at hand, and you're not building the ark, you may want to walk away.

Bad Hand #2 - Junior will be taking over – EVENTUALLY!
Let's say you're in a small, family operated organization, and you're not family. Think your career path may be limited? If they haven't adopted you and you're not marrying someone in the family (for the right reasons), put those cards on the table. Unless you're getting some amazing experience, or some amazing compensation, fold.

Bad Hand #3 - You're about to be promoted – STILL!
You've been busting your butt, performing like crazy, improving processes, killing your results goals, year after year after year! Your promotion is just around the corner – the same corner it was around the year before, and the year before that, and the year before that. How many unfulfilled promises can you take? Is your dignity hanging on the possibility that this might really be the year? Who do you really think is smarter in this game? I know, the world changes. Companies need to downsize, save money, change their promotion criteria, operate in a different regulatory environment, and act on any number of legitimate reasons that result in

you not getting your due. Here's what you are due – a better role in a better company that actually values their talent. Those jobs are out there, those companies are out there, and they would be delighted to have you!

SURVIVAL TIP

Someone may have promised you a rose garden, but roses don't smell like that. Know when to get out! Believe in yourself enough to know that you deserve a future filled with possibility. Find that future!

Part 2
ALL ABOUT ME

Having a boss that sucks is like being in a perpetual emotion machine. The emotions run the gamut and include adjectives like frustration, disappointment, and disbelief. You are left to deal with the carnage, and only you understand its magnitude. You know how it's affecting your life, in and out of the office. Deciding what to do about your situation, to take some action or not, is also difficult. You could make things worse instead of better, or even cost yourself your job. So what are you to do? You hold the only real answer. You need to know yourself well enough to make informed choices. Beyond the details of your situation, here's what you need to know:

1. Strengths – What you're great at.

2. Opportunities – What you're not great at.

3. Values – Values are your core beliefs. They drive all of your choices, decisions, and priorities. There's also no right or wrong to values, and no commonly shared set. Every individual has his or her own values, and yours will not look like anyone else's. You have to answer a question every time your values are in conflict with someone else's. The question is, "Can you tolerate the conflict?" The answer to that question informs the actions you will or won't be able to take in a situation.

4. Tolerances – What can you forgive and forget? You have to create as authentic a relationship as possible with your boss, so knowing the limits of what you can forgive is important. Your tolerance for risk is another consideration. Are you willing to quit your job or get fired? You need to know how far you're willing to push for change.

5. Outcome – You need to be able to describe the resolution you want. Asking for a new boss, for example, may not solve the problem if the problem is that you are not happy with the duties of the job. You need to describe in detail the difference that you want to create.

Perhaps you already have all of this insight in your head. If you do, you're light years ahead of most of us who are struggling with these questions. These are questions that require self-actualization, attentiveness to who we are and what we care about as individuals. We included this section of stories as a guide for deepening our understanding about ourselves. Theses are the stories we learned from, whether we wanted to or not.

CHAPTER 9

OOPS!

A Bryant Story

A sense of humor is part of the art of leadership, of getting along with people, of getting things done.

- Dwight D. Eisenhower

MY BOSS SUCKS

This story is one that I feel I could personally relate about the importance of timely and accurate feedback. It also speaks to the sense of urgency necessary for immediate and sustainable change.

This story brings me back to a time when I was serving in the capacity of deputy sheriff at a local law enforcement agency. I was a member of the S.W.A.T. team and due to that responsibility I was periodically called to respond to high-risk situations ranging from high-risk warrant services to hostage barricade situations. On the day that this particular incident occurred, a few deputies had gone to a trailer with an arrest warrant for a subject who was wanted on outstanding felony charges.

The suspect, not wanting to be apprehended, fled to the back of the trailer and grabbed a shotgun on his way. Being tactically disadvantaged at the time the suspect acquired the weapon, the officers chose not to pursue and set up a perimeter to prevent his escape. There were no other occupants in the trailer. As the situation stood, we had an armed, wanted subject inside a trailer refusing to surrender to authorities. At this point the subject was only posing an immediate threat to himself and potentially individuals in neighboring trailers. Understanding the threat to neighbors and the general public, deputies evacuated the immediate area. The S.W.A.T. team was requested, we responded, and were briefed on the situation.

OOPS!

The standard method to handle an incident of this nature is to exhaust all means to get the subject to come out voluntarily. Entering the location to apprehend the subject is an extreme last resort.

In an effort to get the subject to exit the trailer the decision was made to deploy some tear gas into the trailer. I was elected to deploy that gas using our multi-shot gas gun. I was a firearms instructor, and the multi-shot gas gun was actually new to our department and had never been fired before. Fortunately, as a young Marine I had some experience firing weapons that included an M203 grenade launcher which had a similar sighting system to our newly-acquired multi-shot gas gun.

I took up my position to deliver the first few rounds into the trailer, and did so with complete accuracy. I was very pleased that my assessment of how the sighting system operated was accurate. After deploying those rounds, I needed to move to the other side of the trailer to deploy additional rounds from that side to saturate the interior of the trailer and ensure that there was no safe zone in the trailer into which the suspect could retreat. Getting to the other side of the trailer required me to traverse a hill to the rear of the trailer, staying out of the suspect's line of sight and line of fire, and reposition myself on the far side of the trailer to deliver the additional rounds. Upon repositioning myself in a safe location, I delivered two well-placed shots into a trailer.

I was preparing to fire additional rounds when I heard some unexpected radio traffic. My badge number at the time was 53 and the traffic I heard went like this:

Him: 202 to 53
Me: Go ahead
Him: Check your target

And there wasn't a lot of traffic after that. I had to ponder what he meant. I'm thinking, I just put two well-placed rounds, in the same hole, in a window, in a trailer. As I began to survey the situation, I realized that when I moved to the far side of the trailer to deploy these additional rounds I had temporarily lost sight of the trailer. Apparently, in my excited state, I moved a little too far. When I came up over the hill and so covertly positioned myself to deploy those additional rounds, I had gone beyond that trailer to the next one. Oops! Now, in my defense, all those trailers looked the same. But that radio traffic provided some very valuable feedback. Not quite as timely as it could have been, as I would have preferred to get that feedback before I squeezed off those two rounds. But it was very valuable none-the-less. I then moved to the correct trailer, deployed additional rounds, and the situation was eventually resolved.

The good news is the wrong trailer was an unoccupied rental unit and aside from repairing the window and the need for decontamination, no major damage was done.

I learned some valuable lessons from this scenario. As a leader, I learned the importance of humility and was reminded of that after the incident. Unfortunately for me, it turns out this type of incident is memorable – by many people over long periods of time. It gave me a greater sense of empathy when dealing with peers and subordinates – in understanding that even people who are extremely competent periodically make mistakes. And the important part of all of this is to learn from mistakes and share those mistakes with others so they don't have to travel the same paths that you did to learn the lesson.

SURVIVAL TIP

No matter how skilled we are at performing our jobs, there is always potential to learn something new about ourselves or look at an issue from another viewpoint. Mistakes are generally lessons in disguise, and are designed to prevent us from making a larger mistake in the future. Cherish your mistakes because they represent growth, and always, ALWAYS, check your target.

10
CHAPTER

CLOUD SNEEZES

An Anne Story

The world we have created is a product of our way of thinking.

- Albert Einstein

MY BOSS SUCKS

How well do you know people? I'll take a basic assessment on how well you know anyone – be it your spouse, your kids, your boss, your employees, your parents, friends, anyone. How well do you think you really know them, and how do you know? When was the last time one of them really surprised you?

Last spring Bryant and I were in Colorado at a training program and were out for a walk in the early morning. It was 5:30 or so, dawn was breaking and the clouds were threatening harm. We were a couple of miles away from our destination when we got just the slightest misting of rain, and it lasted for less than a minute. Bryant casually remarked that apparently the clouds just needed to sneeze.

This remark, which I found completely endearing, was a trigger for something more. I know Bryant Halstead well, and on that day I wasn't thinking there was much he could say or do that would surprise me. And on that day, that little cloud-sneezing remark surprised me – a lot!

Just consider who Bryant is. He's a big, strong guy – six feet tall, very athletic and fit, and very smart. He's a man's man – certainly not the man you'd expect to say "cloud sneezes." He does have two small daughters, and living with them and his wife may have contributed somewhat to softening this former Marine, former S.W.A.T. commander, former tri-athlete, as there is virtually no chance that he's become emotionally softer as a result of his business affiliation with me!

CLOUD SNEEZES

It is from this man of all people that I get "cloud sneezes." I'm thinking to myself (and quite possibly aloud since I filter very little with him), "Who are you? Who says, "cloud sneezes" like it's the right thing to do?" And so begins the thinking logic:

1. If Bryant is a man who says something like "cloud sneezes" (which he obviously is because he did), and I didn't expect it from him, what else has he got going on in there that I don't expect?

2. What other surprises has he got waiting for me? And what do I need to do to get at them? I wonder what else he's got squirreled away.

3. And if I don't know that about him – someone I really know well – what do I not know about a bunch of other people I know? Here I've been walking around in this state of satisfaction, this state of arrogant confidence really, about being a good people-person, and then in a sudden bizarre flash I get "cloud sneezes" from Bryant!

4. Holy crap! I better spend some time figuring out what I'm missing in people.

Well, maybe not. Maybe it's not about predicting what everyone has in them. It might instead be about staying open to the possibility, in fact the expectation, that people can and actually should surprise you. People should surprise you with how smart they are, how kind they are, how witty and charming they are. They should surprise you by their choices – what they do and what they don't do. They should surprise you by what they say and what they think, what they know and what they want. They should surprise you by what they love, by what fascinates them, by what makes them laugh and by what makes them cry. They should surprise you by who they are in this moment, who they were before, and who they will become. They should be a constant source of possibility, instead of one of probability. It is in the shift from probability to possibility that people really get to shine. When you are open to all that people could be, most people start to show up all sparkly and full of light. They become sources of joy and inspiration, sources of new hope.

This is my new arrogance. I am confident these days that people will surprise me, sometimes in ways that I like and sometimes in ways that I don't. It is my ambition, my job, my responsibility, to be open to the possibilities of what I will experience. It's like not knowing what's in the wrapped package, and all of the expectation that comes with finding out. Sometimes we get something we love, and sometimes we get a box of raisins (ick, and sorry Aunt Sara!). Sometimes we get more from the experience of opening the package than we do from what's inside, and we always get more from the experience than we would have if our assumptions always proved correct. We get a surprise, and the delight that comes with it.

All this from "cloud sneezes?" Absolutely. All this and more!

SURVIVAL TIP

Surprise yourself today. Do something, say something, be something that you've wanted to do, say, or be. Find one brave thing and do it! And find one thing in someone else. Let it be that surprising thing that you search for in those you know so well.

CHAPTER 11

IT TAKES TACT

An Anne Story

Thought creates the world and then says, "I didn't do it."

- David Bohm

MY BOSS SUCKS

This is the "please-forgive-us-our-faults" chapter. Even with the best of intentions we may not do it right – not as bosses, not as employees, not as people. It also speaks to learning about ourselves, something that is key to leadership success. This is a story about one of my "areas of opportunity." I'll thank you in advance for your patience and your understanding, on behalf of all of us who still have much to learn about who we are. Here's the story:

Yes, it's true, tact, it turns out, is not in my bag of tricks. I have honesty, I have sincerity, and I even have an uncanny ability to create a clever analogy for almost any situation. I am able to, with very little thought or effort, translate complex ideas into actionable possibilities, and I can sometimes be so connected to what you are saying as to finish your sentence with you. What I cannot do – for love or money or if my life depended on it – is reliably communicate in a tactful way.

Tact is truly a mystery to me. I'm not sure of its source or how people think about it or invoke it. I don't know if I've ever used it or had it, and I was thirty-something before I found out I had this gap. That is the saddest news of all – a lifetime of missing this skill and then in a moment, a new understanding of a "real" me that I had never anticipated.

It was over sandwiches, and in the presence of witnesses, that my friend Molly good-naturedly mentioned my remarkable absence of tact. Among the group of peers joining us at that table for lunch, I was the only one surprised by her comment. Others nodded in agreement, eating, drinking, smiling, and generally acknowledging this remark like it was a widely-held fact they had all always known about me. The moment, while perhaps not remarkable in the greater expanse of human history, was earth shattering for me. I had been one person up until that very moment, and was suddenly revealed as another – one I frankly was unprepared to meet and absolutely stunned to see in my own mirror.

I felt it inappropriate at the time to solicit specific examples – afraid perhaps at what else this knowing crowd would present for my consideration. I'm not really sure how many minutes went by before I drew another breath after Molly's remark, which by the way was not intended as news for me. For her it was merely an exercise in expressing the obvious.

One could argue here that Molly's remark may have in and of itself suffered from some absence of tact. I can assure you I don't feel sufficiently qualified to know. I can also assure you that people generally don't tell you when you've been tactless in their presence. You hear about it later – in the form of hurt feelings, or from someone else, or on your 360 appraisal comments, or in the root of a frustration that appears much later in your relationship. It turns out that not having great tact can be damaging to relationships. I'm suspecting now that the intention at the core of tact may be deep personal concern for the relationship – a specific intention to care for the person with whom you are interacting, and the relationship that the two of you are building. I suspect this because it has occurred to me after much consideration that there are some relationships that I believe have evolved to pure trust. They exist for me with people who are so important to me, who I love so much, that I want to guard their emotional well being with my life! I'm learning that while this state of pure trust may be how the relationships exist in my mind, I need to overtly evidence that love by being especially attentive to caring for their feelings. This is the part that for me takes conscious attention and work. It isn't naturally occurring in my automatic relationship activities, and that makes it a problem.

I have a long way to go in learning and doing this work around tact, this work around intention, around caring all the time in all the right ways. It's work I value highly, and I am eternally hopeful that this whole tact thing is "coachable," that I have a chance at getting better at it. And mostly I hope that the people who I love the most will be patient with me, and will always know that I intend to love them full out, and that my absence of tact is just that – the absence of tact and something that I'm trying to fix.

SURVIVAL TIP

Embrace your weaknesses, understand them, and then work on your strengths. Our strengths are the areas in which we can gain the greatest ground. We would never ask a gifted cellist to learn how to play the guitar in order to be a great musician. We would ask the cellist to continue to practice the cello. The same applies to you and your gifts.

12
CHAPTER

MAKING IT STICK

An Anne and Bryant Story

To command is to serve, nothing more and nothing less.

- Andre Malraux

MY BOSS SUCKS

This is a true story of a dear friend and former co-worker of ours, and it is with her permission that we share it with you. It has to do with bad bosses (good news since this is what our book is about), good bosses, boss egos, truth, and reality. It also has to do with Post-it® brand notes (credit where due to 3M – www.Post-it.com. We are eternally grateful).

Our friend Kristine is brilliant at her job – period. No one disputes this. No one argues whether or not Kristine can accomplish what she commits to get done. No one argues with her process. Kristine has sometimes been "accused" of something that resembles over-honesty – if there is such a thing. She takes very little in the way of crap from anyone – regardless of their rank, position, title, or financial standing. She has passion for her work. She is committed to the success of the enterprise. She is genuine and authentic. Most importantly, she makes it her business to ensure that the company she works for does right by the people who work there. In short, she cares about all the right things and does all the right stuff. She is by any standard an exceptional employee.

Kristine worked for 22 bosses at one company in a seven-year period. That's not a typo – twenty-two bosses. Hmmmm... What's wrong with that picture? Many of Kristine's 21 former bosses don't work for the company anymore, which is good news for the company as well as for Kristine. Most of them weren't that good at being bosses. They might have had other great strengths, but as bosses they just weren't all that.

So that's the set-up - Kristine's training ground at this particular company is 21 not-so-good bosses. The 22nd (FINALLY) is by Kristine's high standard a GREAT boss. He is smart, open, funny, balanced, actually does some work, and is able to ideate possibilities – answers that the team might not have arrived at on their own. Kristine holds a high bar, and Michael (aka Boss Number 22) delivers.

Here's where the Post-it® notes come in. Once a week, as a matter of standard practice, Kristine and Michael have a meeting. It is Kristine's standard approach (much to Michael's chagrin) to bring with her something to write with and some-thing to write on. The thing she chooses to write on for these weekly meetings with her boss is a Post-it® note. In fact, it's a really small Post-it® note. It's one that makes Michael uncomfortable.

You understand, of course, that the message Kristine sends with her really small Post-it® note pad-of-choice is that if Michael were to have anything important to say – anything important enough that Kristine should need to write it down - she would be able to do so in its entirety on a really small Post-it® note. Talk about mak-ing a message "stick!" You go girl! ;)

Michael, in recovering from the slight of the really small Post-it® note phenomenon, takes up the challenge. He commits to finding things sufficiently important to convey that Kristine will find herself desiring – nay demanding – a larger piece of paper. And remember we said he was funny? He was fortunate enough to find in his travels an itty-bitty pad of paper – something doll-house sized. He usurped it and stowed it in his desk for his next one-on-one meeting with Kristine. His presentation to Kristine of the itty-bitty pad of paper accomplished a number of things:

1. It articulated to Kristine that he got her message – even though she hadn't expressly set out to communicate it.

2. It made them BOTH laugh – ALWAYS a good thing.

3. It created a moment – a connection between the two of them – an emotional experience. These things are the foundations of great relationships.

HALSTEAD salutes Kristine and Michael! Kristine for being true to herself and the situation, "Look mister, I've had enough of these meetings and enough bad bosses to know that all I'll ever need to write on when you're talking is a really small Post-it® note pad." Michael for being true to himself and to his talented employee, "Look lady, I'm onto your game and I'm not going to be that kind of boss!"

We can all think of a number of other ways this sticky situation could have played out, and it is the wit, the charm, and the intelligence of the two people involved who ensured the most positive outcome. Cheers to you both!

SURVIVAL TIP

Just try to keep your subconscious from making a point! If your mouth isn't saying it, some other part of your body is. We communicate to people in a myriad of different ways, and people communicate to us in even more. Pay attention to what you're "saying." And it's important to "note" that every now and again a really good boss comes along. You and a good boss can create a magical relationship, and some powerful business results. Hold a high bar for good bosses, and help make them better. Get yourself some really small Post-it® notes to carry the message, and see what happens.

CHAPTER 13

PLAN B

A Bryant Story

If you listen to your fears, you will die never knowing what a great person you might have been.

- Robert H. Schuller

Let's talk about the difference between managing and leading. Most organizations are full of people who are competent to manage things, but when we talk about management, how many people are able to inspire others? To help people achieve things above the norm, to identify qualities about themselves that they didn't even know existed?

How many years have we been talking about the difference between leading and managing? Too many, and most people still don't get it. We think the best way to think about it is like this: you lead people and you manage stuff. You don't need to lead stuff – it can't be led, and people shouldn't be managed – they don't like it. We don't need world managers; we need world leaders.

Let's create some awareness of vocabulary and let's start with those two terms: leadership and management. Let's create some understanding of the difference between those two terms and the desire to use them in the right context. Leadership is about people. Management is about stuff. If your company is full of managers, people who manage people like they're stuff, you just need to manage them right on out of the company and get some leaders in there. Leaders create emotions in people, emotions that make people want to excel at their jobs.

I've worked with a number of people over the course of my career that were incredibly talented in their process skills, the technical aspects of a given job, but you could put their leadership skill - their people skill - into a thimble. Unfortunately, the larger part of their job required leadership, and they just didn't have the skills to be effective. So how did they ever get promoted? What do organizations look for in the people they promote? They typically look for people who are top performers in their current jobs, people who have strong technical skills or intelligence. Companies rarely look for people who are able to inspire people and develop relationships. How do you test for that? Most companies have no idea.

What about the person who gets promoted and does have the skills, they're doing a great job, but they don't enjoy it? They actually miss aspects of their old role, and their promotions have taken them away from the day-to-day work that they used to love.

It's been our experience in presenting leadership development programs to companies that at least one leader in every program approaches us with this issue. It's not an uncommon situation. In fact, we believe that it's more common than most companies know. We think the roots of this problem actually run deep – into the values of American society. Our culture pushes people to strive for the next promotion, the next rung on the ladder. Heaven forbid you shouldn't want to take that step, that promotion wouldn't be something you'd want to consider.

What do you do with those people -- the people who got promoted into a leadership role and shouldn't have, and those who got promoted and don't like it? In a lot of ways they are the same person. I'm not sure they should be viewed any differently. Both categories of people had the skills and were well-respected, enabling them to get promoted to start with. An effort needs to be made to determine where within the organization their talents, knowledge, and skills can be used in a way that benefits them and the company. Currently, many of these folks are left with what they believe is the only option – to leave their current organization and go find a role in another business that may be better suited to their skills and preferences.

My military and law enforcement background enables me to reflect back on various high-risk missions. I was responsible for planning many of those missions and we would never consider undertaking an operation like that without having a contingency plan. In these cases, lives were at stake. Why would a company, or one of their star employees, undertake something like a role change or significant promotion and not have a contingency plan? Lives are at stake – a lot of them. The lives of the leaders who are getting promoted are at stake as well as those of the people for whom they are responsible, not to mention those with whom they'll have daily interaction. You've got to have a Plan B. I wish we were in a position to tell you what that Plan B should be, but there is no cookie cutter solution. I think it may be more of an individual solution specific to each organization and each situation. Perhaps there could be a probationary period, such as when people are newly hired. Perhaps companies should create a solution that stacks the odds in favor of both the company and the employee. Each needs a plan to fall back on in case the new role isn't a good fit for either.

Solving this problem is important from an operational success standpoint. How effective are those leaders who are stuck in positions for which they're not well suited? Again, some of these leaders may think they are well suited when they actually are not. Those you have to treat differently. You need to bring it to their attention that this isn't a great role for them, and that they could make a significant contribution to the corporation in another way if you could give them the coaching and the opportunity. The person who is stuck in the role and doesn't like it needs the same type of an out that allows them to maintain their dignity. Across industries we are preparing to deal with senior level people who will be exiting the workforce in the next 10 years. Where will companies get their experienced talent after that? There are plenty of initiatives to get older workers back into the workforce and to maintain them longer, however there's a key element missing in the equation. Companies are letting key talent walk out the door because there aren't systems in place to take care of people as they ascend the career ladder, and ultimately end up in roles that don't suit them well.

While there are a number of mathematical equations about the cost of recruiting and training new talent, there is universal agreement that finding, hiring, and training new people is more expensive than keeping the talent that you have. Why wouldn't organizations be motivated to develop processes through which they could invest in the development of your talent, allow you to try out new roles, and have an alternate plan in case the new role isn't a great fit for either party? It just makes sense that companies would want to find a way to optimize their existing

SURVIVAL TIP

You're not stuff, so don't let yourself be treated that way. You're a valuable asset to the organization. Work for one that treats you that way. Appreciate that the future has more than one possible outcome, and you get to choose.

CHAPTER 14

FALL OUT

A Bryant Story

Everything you want is on the other side of fear.

- Jack Canfield

MY BOSS SUCKS

Context – I'm 14 years into my law enforcement career. I've accomplished everything I wanted to accomplish. I've been promoted through the ranks to the position of Captain and I find myself banging my head into a glass ceiling for upward promotion. I'm also banging my head against a brick wall when it comes to influencing positive and significant change in a stagnant organization masquerading as one that is proactive. It is technologically advanced and intellectually challenged. These people have the courage to go up against a violent offender armed with a deadly weapon and at the same time lack the moral courage to do what's right for their employees.

The choices that I had were to continue to bump my head and risk suffering permanent "injury" or change something – do something different. Changing my boss would require some sort of mystical abilities that I didn't possess. I'd actually already tried that and learned that I couldn't turn water into wine. I made a choice, and one of the things I learned is that you just never know how your choice impacts others. Here's a story about the courage of my convictions, and how it affected someone else.

Toward the end of my career with the Sheriff's Office, I made a somewhat unconventional move. My dissatisfaction with my role as the Captain of the Criminal Investigations Division caused me significant inner turmoil. Several things were happening in my life, I was starting a leadership development business, and I realized that it was important for me to make a change that would let me be more satisfied and happy with my job. I requested that I be reassigned to a previous role that was two steps back – the role of patrol shift supervisor (or first sergeant). The focus of this story is on something that happened as a result of making that move.

A couple of weeks after I made the decision and went back to the position of first sergeant, a first sergeant assigned to Criminal Investigations (my former division) decided that he wasn't happy in his role, and requested that he be reassigned to his prior role as a detective. He had similar issues and concerns in his role as a first sergeant that I had as a Captain. The stress and unhappiness of the job were causing adverse effects on his health. He'd already had one heart attack and was knocking on the door of another. He was engaged to be married, and sensitive to statistics about law enforcement officers who worked until retirement only to pass away shortly thereafter – not a fate he wanted for himself.

Hearing that the first sergeant had stepped back to detective, I went to talk to him to see how he was doing and to understand more about his decision to step back. He shared his concerns with me. I asked him whether or not he would have made that decision if I had not made my decision to step back. He said no – he would not have made the same decision. He said that he didn't know whether he could handle the "fall-out" of making a decision like that, but because I had done it I had actually paved the way for him to do it, and made it okay.

For those of you not familiar with law enforcement, the "fall out" from stepping back in your career is significant. Stepping back isn't something that is normally done voluntarily. People automatically assume that when an officer moves backward on the hierarchy, it indicates that he or she has done something wrong. No matter what an officer says, there will always be those individuals who won't believe that there wasn't something wrong that actually caused the move. If they don't feel like they're getting a good enough story, some folks have no problem spreading rumors about why it happened. Some of the stories that people come up with to explain this action! I only wish that the people who engage in creating and spreading rumors would have the self-control to redirect that creative energy toward more productive agendas.

The detective went on to say that I may have saved his life by opening that door for him – by enabling him to make that decision. Hearing him say that left me with a lump in my throat. This guy is a 20+ year law enforcement veteran. He's been involved in violent situations, not unlike some of the situations I've been involved in, and he says with utmost sincerity that the move I made enabled him to make a move that could have saved his life. That's just powerful! What a feeling to know that you can have such an impact. I didn't save his life – he saved his own life – by his conscious decision to make a change. All I did was open a door – he's the one who had to walk through it. When I think about that whole situation, and how if I had gone back to the role of first sergeant and not liked it, and even been completely miserable, I would have been okay with that, just knowing the action I took created such a profound reaction in the universe.

The bottom line here is that you don't often have the foresight to see what your actions may allow others to do. Truly, as a leader, you have the ability to influence the lives of the people around you. You can inspire them. You can open doors for them that you don't even realize, just by being who you are. When you demonstrate that you have the courage to do what's right for you even when it's not what is expected, it is a great example for others.

SURVIVAL TIP

Follow your heart. You know the best thing to do for you. Do that and it will be the best thing you can do for others. Be the leader you were meant to be.

CHAPTER 15

GOAT RODEO

An Anne Story

It may be hard for an egg to turn into a bird: it would be a jolly sight harder for it to learn to fly while remaining an egg. We are like eggs at present. And you cannot go on indefinitely just being an ordinary, decent egg. We must be hatched or go bad.

- C.S. Lewis

MY BOSS SUCKS

That's it! My boss has had it! He is a brilliant man and the best boss I've ever had. I had just given him the next piece of bad news in a long bad-news story that we are helpless to change. My boss lost it, but not in a yelling-screaming-have-you-lost-your-mind-crazy sort of way. More in a quiet-head-shaking-we're-too-damn-smart-to-be-doing-this sort of way. He plunked down in one of the chairs around the conference table, dropped his head into his hands, and said: "My life is a goat rodeo."

Now, I'm from Virginia, part of the Washington D.C. metropolitan area, and I admit proudly and without shame that until that very moment I had little (read NO) goat rodeo experience. I had never participated in one and never been an observer of one. I didn't know any goat rodeo people. I didn't think my boss was one of them and I knew that I wasn't. I asked for more insight (because how could you not), however no specific goat rodeo details were forthcoming.

There I was, clearly part of something (albeit newly named) that at least resembled in my boss' mind a goat rodeo. Up until that point I had been having a completely normal day, and from that moment forward I was left to ponder what precisely it was that rendered my beloved boss' current state of being analogous to a goat rodeo? How frustrating, bizarre, and out of control things must be for "goat rodeo" to be what you are living, feeling, and saying out loud? And here I thought it was just Thursday.

There are times in our lives when things are just beyond our control. People are doing whatever people need to do. Processes are doing whatever processes need to do. The events of the day are whatever the events are. And the result of the people being, processes doing, and events unfolding, is that the earth spins on its own axis, with or without your approval or consent. It becomes your job to make some sort of sense of the craziness, some sort of reason from the inane. It is your job to turn the goat rodeo into something that makes sense. So let me know how you do with that.

Creating order from chaos takes a plan, and it takes the right mindset to execute the plan. It takes a sort of irrational confidence, a willingness to walk into the void armed with your good sense, your experience, and a flashlight with extra batteries (and perhaps some snacks). It takes courage. It takes a sense of humor, plenty of flexibility, and a strong set of values. Those values could be the only clear boundaries you've got in that void, those and a good sense of where you'd like to come out on the other side. Mostly though, it takes wanting to do it. Yep - it mostly takes caring enough about your boss, your co-workers, your business, and your customers that you'll do what it takes to get through to the other side. We'll call these things "commitment," and that's what I'd signed on for. I signed on to do whatever it takes to make this business work. I signed on to create a different kind of industry, a different kind of company. I signed on to create products that would take care of people in a way that doesn't exist today, and I believe SO MUCH in the possibility that I'll do whatever it takes. Commitment.

Not every boss, not every company, not every job creates a strong sense of commitment in people. It's your responsibility to get yourself in one that does it for you. You win... we all win. We all win when each one of us is in a role where we can make a significant contribution, one that makes us feel good about what we do, how hard we try, and what we deliver. We are all better served when we can all work with a genuine sense of commitment.

A couple of months have passed and you should know that I'm getting better at working the goat rodeo. I like the craziness of it, the wild-west-ness of a new frontier. I like not knowing how the events will turn out (or even necessarily what the events are). I like the risk, the bright lights, and the unknown. I'm in. Commitment.

SURVIVAL TIP

Find work that stretches you, that takes you out of your comfort zone enough that you can grow. Find it in a place that you want to be, doing things you want to be doing, with people you want to be doing it with. Never saddle up for less than your best ride.

16
CHAPTER

COWBOY UP

An Anne Story

Courage is being scared to death – but saddling up anyway.

- John Wayne

If you're reading this book, it's because you currently have, used to have, know, or have been a bad boss. Maybe all of the above – in which case we're truly sorry! Maybe you've had more bad bosses than you can count, in which case we should chat because the problem may be more about you than about them. Whatever the case, let's acknowledge how difficult it is to exist in a situation where what you're doing for a living is encumbered by who you're doing it with. Having a bad boss sucks! Doing something about it is altogether different.

Bad bosses are sadly much more the rule than they are the exception. We need to call out that while few bosses start out to be bad bosses, way too few are as concerned as they should be with getting better at it. Way too few are taking the initiative to learn and grow – to become a better leader, and there's a reason for that. It turns out that there's a process that happens inside our brains that makes it difficult for people to want to change. It has to do with ways that we learn – ways that our brains seek to order new information inside the hierarchy of existing information. We're chemically wired for change to be difficult, so change is something we have to seek out with intention. We need to go after it to make it happen.

Becoming a better boss is all about wanting to change. It's about having the courage to change. It takes courage to learn what works and what doesn't, to understand the values that are in play in any given situation, and to have the foresight and the historical perspective to keep your head when emotion (read fear) wants to carry you away. It takes courage to seek information, to seek understanding, and to persistently drive to achieve results, especially when the traditional methods don't work.

Being a bad boss is a symptom of a bigger problem, and there are three lead contenders:

1. Values (I don't care what kind of boss I am for you.)
2. Limited self-awareness/denial/arrogance (I'm a great boss!)
3. Fear/good intention (I'm doing the best that I can.)

All of these symptoms have in common the absence of courage and the absence of commitment to the role of boss – the unwillingness to seek insight and make attendant change.

If the bigger problem is conflict of values, you could be in a tough spot. There is no right or wrong for values. People have the values they have and they don't easily change their values. Changing values takes awareness, a powerful new awareness typically created by an emotional experience.

If the bigger problem is limited self-awareness, it may be enough just to point out to the boss that their boss behavior isn't having the effect they'd intended. It's like needing to tell someone that they have something stuck in their teeth. Someone needs to tell them. Remember, it's your obligation to offer feedback. If you know and they don't know, please tell them. The truth might hurt, but it won't hurt nearly so much as finding out that an employee you trusted knew something that could help you and they chose not to share it with you.

Your own fear is the most challenging opportunity of all. Bryant always uses this quote from Jack Canfield, "Everything you want is on the other side of fear." The magic part is less perhaps the getting past fear part and more perhaps the wanting to part. You need to identify what you're afraid of, name it, face it, and move past it. It's the wanting to get past the fear that will get this done – the willingness to actually cross the line.

So what then do we expect of you – all of you who struggle under the "leadership" of the bad-boss masses? We expect you to step up and help fill the void. We expect you to be courageous when those around you can't find it for themselves. We expect you to practice what you would preach if it were your role to do so. We expect you to find a way to help. And that takes plenty of courage of your very own!

Your courage will come in finding ways to have conversations that are productive and will move your manager to a different perspective. It will come in finding ways to deliver feedback that may be difficult. It will come in recognizing that change is difficult, that not everyone can handle it, and that even when change does happen it happens in spurts and is rife with the imperfection of learning. Your courage will come from finding in your professional strife your own personal lesson – the thing that you can learn from your situation. Your courage will come in knowing that you did all you could do in that situation – that you left all you had on the field of battle – win or lose.

That's what we mean when we say "Cowboy up!" We mean that it is our individual and collective mission to help through the battle all of those who can not help themselves. The Marines have a whole culture based on this concept. Their commitment, their promise, is to leave no man behind. That culture in HALSTEAD-speak is "Cowboy up!" Leave no boss behind. It is your accountability to do EVERYTHING you can to help that boss improve – BECAUSE you can. And you have to know that leaving no boss behind doesn't mean never leaving the job. Bosses learn from that, too (sometimes we need to talk with our feet). If it is in the best interest of your contribution and your boss' learning for you to leave the role – leave the role. If your boss has to fire you because you keep trying to help him or her learn and improve – get fired. There will be other roles, and trust us when we tell you that other employers will highly value your efforts and your intentions.

Bad bosses need great employees even more desperately than great bosses do. We suspect that it's no accident that you ended up with this bad boss. You clearly have something unique and special that you can offer him or her. You have perspectives from which they can learn, and that's a powerful asset.

SURVIVAL TIP

Cowboy up! Do everything you can to help your boss become a better boss. Cowboy up also means that you do what it takes for your own personal development. It means you seek feedback, learn from experiences, and persist in getting the job done well. Here's our question for you: have you done all YOU can do? If the answer is no, then get moving. It's time for you to cowboy up!

17
CHAPTER

COW ENERGY

An Anne Story

Ideologies separate us. Dreams and anguish bring us together.

- Eugene Ionesco

Whether you are the boss or the employee, think about how this story about cows could relate to you. (No really – we're starting with cows and we're ending up with leadership. It might sound bizarre, but it works.)

Picture this: Bryant and I are in a training program and I'm on a horse (that I can barely ride), with a team of three others (equally as adept) and we are collectively tasked with moving some number of calves around a ring away from their herd and into a pen. This is, in my humble opinion, the quintessential definition of you-have-lost-your-ever-loving-mind. There is, again in my humble opinion, no way in hell we're moving these cattle anywhere with intention. But this is the mission with which we are tasked. And we've apparently got as much time as it takes to figure out how to get this done. We've already watched ONE wrangler do it, (there are four of us) and he made it look simple. Now it's simply up to us to do the same thing.

First of all, I already know that I have to believe we can succeed in order for us to have any chance of succeeding, so I start working on the shift in my mental attitude. Done. I also know that I can step up as a leader and help create a positive result. Done. It turns out that there are a few things I don't know, especially about cows, and here the learning begins.

Cow Fact Number One: Cows, it turns out, want to stay with the herd. Safety in numbers? I don't know. Diminished chances of being caught assuming some cow in the herd is slower than another? I don't know. But cow facts are cow facts. Cows want to get back to the herd. Period.

Cow Fact Number Two: This is the real killer. You can't succeed if you block the cows' energy. WHAT?!?! Are you friggin' kidding me? Did this dusty old dude ranch wrangler just insert some actual metaphysical thing into team cattle penning? Let me make myself clear – cow facts are cow facts – don't block the cows' energy. Period.

What this means in application is that cows need a place to go. You need to keep pushing them forward, and you can't block their forward path. If you block their forward path, they "squirt" out and then things turn into a real mess that, in my experience, requires expert wranglers to recover. Preventing cow squirting requires serious attention to cow energy. You really do have to keep a forward path open for the cows - one that they recognize as forward and that they think is big enough. Otherwise - squirting - and a myriad of associated disasters!

I'm still struck, months after this cow energy lesson, by the compelling relationship that moving cattle has to leadership – in fact to interpersonal relationships in general. While I'm not completely convinced that every person wants to stay with the "herd," I totally believe that we must all pay serious attention to not blocking

145

someone else's energy. We want to keep pushing people forward, challenging them to realize their potential and ensuring that they have a path that they know is big enough for them.

Just think about the implications of this – about what it would be like for you to stay out of the way of the energy of your kids, your spouse, and the people who work with you. Think what it would mean to push people forward in a way that was sensitive to their forward path. I find thinking about it just amazing! Imagine the power of actually doing it!

So I now know that cow facts are cow facts. Period. And it appears that some cow facts are people facts, too. Prove it for yourself in answering this question: Do you feel like your boss is blocking your energy? Do you have a lot more to contribute - creativity, skills, talents? Are these things valued? Is there a forward path for you in your company, and if so, is it big enough? Or are you thinking about "squirting" - running amuck and taking a gang of friends with you when you go?

If you're the boss, think about this: What percentage of your team is watching the clock and what have you done to contribute to their state of being? How have you blocked their energy, forced them to be in places they didn't want to be, forced them to go the way you wanted them to go and get there the way you wanted them to get there? Guess what? We know from watching those cows that your people are picking their moment. They're watching you, and the moment they get a chance they're squirting – they'll be GONE and you'll need more than the help of professional wranglers to get them back. You don't even have the benefit of a fence. You will be on your own and your cows will no longer be with you. You'll be alone in the empty pen – up on your high horse. You have a choice though. You can either learn to enjoy the view from the saddle, or learn to manage energy in a productive way – a positive, constructive, help-people-be-what-they-are sort of way. Start doing that and you'll suddenly find that you won't need a whole crew to lead those folks. One lone wrangler with the right skill and the right level of attention to the right things can get it all done – in a way that everyone feels good about. Cow energy – people energy – there's a lesson here!

SURVIVAL TIP

It's your energy and it can't be blocked unless you let it. Make sure you always have a clear path forward, and clear the way for others while you're at it.

CHAPTER 18

THE UNREASONABLE MAN

A Bryant Story

Hell, there are no rules here – we're trying to accomplish something.

- Thomas A. Edison

There is a quote from George Bernard Shaw that we use in our HALSTEAD leadership development training. The quote reads like this: "The reasonable man adapts himself to the world, but the unreasonable man tries to adapt the world to him – therefore all progress depends on the unreasonable man." There may be times when the relative reasonableness of your behavior has everything to do with the situation in which you find yourself. Please allow me to share with you a story about a situation in which I behaved somewhat "unreasonably," and influenced change nonetheless.

This story takes me back to a situation that occurred when I was a lieutenant in the Sheriff's Office assigned to the patrol division. The major for the Sheriff's Office had a reputation of being the ultimate procrastinator and unwilling to make a decision. His standard response for most any situation revolved around needing more information to make the decision, or needing more time to think about it. It was the running joke around the command staff in the Sheriff's Office that if there was a project that you didn't want to complete, just do your part and send it to the major. It was guaranteed that the project would "die in assembly."

While the specifics of this incident are not important, it was another in a string of incidences in which the major failed to make a decision, stating that this was something he needed more time to think about and for which he needed more information. It was a widely held opinion that this was not an appropriate response in this situation. It became clear to me that the major had all of the information needed; what he lacked was the confidence to decide. He failed to make a decision and his failure spun me up. This frustrated me and I was feeling how the people under me would be feeling. You can do all that you can do to a certain point. When there are decisions to be made that have to be made by individuals of higher organizational rank, those individuals have a responsibility to make those decisions -- decisions in this case that affect the lives of others. Your individual fear, or lack of confidence in your abilities to decide, cannot be allowed to inhibit that responsibility.

By way of context, let me explain that in a paramilitary hierarchy the chain of command is the method by which issues or concerns get escalated and addressed. While there are appropriate situations where an officer could circumvent the chain of command, this situation was not one. The options that remain in taking on issues, concerns, or processes that aren't working (in this case the decision process at the level of major) are limited and politically charged. There are no processes by which performance feedback is solicited or provided from sources other than the officer's direct manager, nor are there formal processes by which organizational lessons are learned. This is the backdrop that framed my actionable options. My captain's unwillingness or inability to take the issue up with his manager (the major) meant that I was blocked on the chain of command, and I thereby needed to end-run the political proprieties to effect change. Here's what I decided to do.

In an effort to vent some of my frustration I created a quote that I posted on a shelf in my office. While I'm imprecise on the exact verbiage, the net effect of the quote was "More lives will be lost on the field of battle due to the inability to make a decision than will be lost in making the wrong decision." I didn't direct this quote to anyone in particular. It said just that. No one's name was associated with it, and I felt much better after I wrote it. I shared this quote with my captain and another captain within the command staff, and they both agreed that it was a very appropriate representation of the issue that we were facing. You might be thinking that this was a passive–aggressive way to handle this situation and you are right! I don't think that this would be the appropriate way to act in all situations; however, in an environment that does not encourage open, honest, and authentic communication, it might be necessary to get a point across.

A few days went by and I was called into the Sheriff's office because the major had come across this quote in my office. While it didn't have his name on it, the major had figured out that this was directed at him. Now why was that? If his name wasn't on it, how did he figure out it was about him? Could it be that he realized that this was an inadequacy that he had and it completely spun him up for someone to point it out to him? It's also interesting that he took it to the Sheriff. Apparently he didn't have the wherewithal to decide how to handle it (go figure). He was two levels above me in the chain of command and had to call "the Sheriff (dad?)" in to help him. (More evidence of incompetence? I think so!)

THE UNREASONABLE MAN

As I sat in the Sheriff's office, with the captain (my supervisor) and endured the berating from the Sheriff about how inappropriate it was for me to post this quotation, I had to ask the major why he thought this quote was about him. It was interesting that this seemed to anger him more, but I thought it was a completely legitimate question. I remind you, his name was not associated with the quote at all. The sad ending to this was that he never really answered that question. What did happen, though, was that my captain was punished by not being allowed to attend a critical training opportunity that could have advanced his abilities to serve our community and our team.

The captain was held accountable for my choice of action, when ultimately my behavior was a symptom of the true problem. The accountability should have been directed at the major and at the Sheriff, because it was the major's inadequacies that brought us to that point in the first place. The Sheriff, responsible for the actions (or inactions) of the major, was either ignorant to the situation or unwilling to deal with it, for whatever reason. Sadly, I was the only member of the command staff to have either the courage or the ignorance (I'm not sure which) to throw gasoline on that fire and bring the point to light. It was interesting to watch some of the positive changes in the way that the major operated from that point forward. Clearly the Sheriff had realized that there was truth in what was being said and in his own way initiated steps to deal with it.

The bottom line here is that as a leader you sometimes have to be willing to engage in unconventional (or what some consider unacceptable) behavior to get your point across. It's unfortunate that the captain was denied a training opportunity that he deserved, but the organization ultimately benefited by bringing this problem to the surface and forcing a change in the way the major did business.

SURVIVAL TIP

Be brave enough to put it out there, have the courage to be unreasonable, and be smart about it. Tremendous results can be obtained through shock and awe.

CHAPTER 19

NOW WHAT?

Dream no small dreams for they have no power to move the hearts of men.

- Johann Wolfgang von Goethe

All right, we agree. Your boss sucks! Now what? What are you going to do about it? The choices are yours and the power is yours. Consider the circumstances in which you find yourself and choose what course of action you want to take. We think there are three obvious choices:

1. Victim Approach - Allow yourself to be a victim, to be cynical, to suck it up and stick it out in your current circumstance and do nothing.

2. Reframe or Change - Change yourself or your situation. Change how you view your situation (reframe), change how you act in your situation (and thereby create a different result), or simply leave your job.

3. Help Your Boss Change - Invest in changing your boss. Take on the challenge of helping him or her become a better boss.

Each of these choices has its own strengths and weaknesses. Each requires some input from you that you may or may not be comfortable with, and each has some outcomes that are predictable and some that are not. So let's examine your options.

Victim Approach

Let's say you choose to reside comfortably in the role of victim, nay martyr. Let's say cynical is a position you've grown comfortable with and all you really want to do is share that perspective with others. Misery does, after all, love company. Let's say you decide that happiness at work either isn't all that important to you or isn't attainable – that you are destined to be miserable at your job whatever your job is, and with whomever your boss is. Let's say your boss will always suck because he or she will always be your boss, and the mere notion of even having a boss is your real issue.

We say here-here! Cheers to the victim! You've chosen the prize behind Door Number One - your path to "disengaged clock-watcher," which, according to the Gallup organization, comfortably places you with 71% of the American work-force. We'll avoid the temptation to talk macroeconomics – the global economic impact of 71% of the U.S. workforce performing at what we have to assume is significantly less than their collective potential – and talk about what this means for you. Here are some questions that you can answer for yourself:

1. What does it mean for you to choose a path that will never make you happy?
2. What does it say about the kind of person you are if there are choices you could make that could improve the situation (for yourself and potentially for others) and you are unwilling to make them?
3. What does it say about the rest of your life's choices? Are you choosing to suck it up in other areas of your life as well?
4. Can you sustain this existence over the long run? Is this creating the kind of life on which you'll want to reflect in your old age? Is this the life you will have been proud to have lived?

Reframe or Change

Our lives are made up of our thoughts. We can see situations as problems or we can see them as opportunities. We can see them as good or bad, right or wrong, and we have complete control over our view. What that means is that we also have complete control over changing our view. We can look for the positives in our situation – what we are learning, and how we might benefit from the examples our boss is setting for us. We can appreciate the people we work with or the type of work we get to do. And if we are unable to find a single valuable perspective we can change it all. Take the opportunity to learn as much as you can, perform as well as you can, build your professional network, and change roles within your company or change jobs.

Changing jobs may or may not solve your problem. On the other side of this change is a big unknown: how well will you like your new boss, your new peer group, your new company, and your new work? Will the change be worth the risk and upheaval, especially if you need to relocate? Better the devil you know in some cases, which means you may be better off in the situation you understand and know how to navigate within. When you start something new, you can plan to spend the first six months to a year just figuring out whether or not the change was the right thing to do – for you and your family. Know what you're getting into on this one.

The statement, "We serve the world best by doing the thing we love the most" plays so strongly in this situation. Would your relationship with your new boss matter if you were doing the thing you loved the most? Is there a way to figure out what you love to do and start doing it? The answer is yes – there is absolutely a way. Send us an e-mail – info@halstead.bz - and we will connect you with some resources, at least some places to start that will help you on this journey.

Help Your Boss Change

Let us assume that your boss is coming at his or her job with positive intentions – that he or she really does care about doing a "good job" and would choose to do it well if offered the choice between doing it well and doing it badly. Our first question then is does your boss know how you are feeling? What have you done in the way of providing your boss with developmental feedback? Whether or not your company has a formal process for feedback, you have considerable influence over how your boss performs, especially if you choose to take on the role of helping him or her improve. Here are some tips to providing someone (your boss, your wife, your kids, anyone) with feedback.

1. Create space for imperfect execution.

The mere mention of the word "feedback" typically has negative connotations. Most of us are not practiced in the art of receiving feedback – either good or bad – and neither are we practiced in the art of giving it. You can get around this by creating some grace – ask for permission to be awkward, to do it imperfectly, to learn as you go, to be valued for the effort as much as for the result. This opens the door to a productive conversation.

2. Realize what you get paid to do.

As much as you might not like to hear it, part of all of our jobs is to help make our bosses successful. That doesn't mean we need to kiss anyone's anything, suck up, or play political games. It does mean that we need to understand our individual role in the success of the team, and do everything we can to make the team successful. It also means that we need to understand our boss – at least appreciate the complexities of the world he or she plays in and be flexible in adapting to his or her style of managing. Management styles differ, especially along the lines of communication preferences, decision-making preferences, approaches to solving problems, and methods of interacting.

3. Offer constructive feedback

Feedback should be about providing your boss with information he or she can use to behave in a different way. Affecting that outcome (a change in your boss' behavior) requires some investment on your part – the careful design of your feedback. Here are some guidelines for good feedback:

- Make it helpful
- Be direct and honest
- Be descriptive and specific
- Be timely

Feedback should be positive as well as negative – giving both is more helpful than giving all of one or all of the other. Giving both makes you more credible, and frames a relationship between you and your boss that is genuine and based on trust. Remember that blame is not the same as feedback. Feedback really is a conversation that seeks to positively influence your boss' behavior, and the same should be said about your boss' feedback for you.

There are your choices – be a victim, change, or help to change your boss. You know your situation, your boss, and your abilities and willingness to act. You decide how you want to manage this relationship, what you want it to mean to you, and what you're willing to invest to make it better. It's up to you to choose.

SURVIVAL TIP!

You ALWAYS have the power to choose. Not choosing is a choice. Your circumstance is your circumstance because you have chosen it. Choose an outcome that you can be happy with. Live well!

SURVIVAL TIP
SUMMARY

This book is part storybook and part survival guide. Here's a consolidated look at the survival tips from each chapter that you can use as a quick reference.

Chapter 1
I'M RUBBER AND YOU'RE GLUE

By Bryant

Be courageous and offer feedback to your boss. They'll never get better at receiving it if you don't teach them and maybe they'll appreciate your candor. If you have information that can help someone improve, it's your obligation to share it. Also, remember to ask for feedback if you're not getting it. It's valuable. Feedback is positive!

Chapter 2
DANCING BEARS

By Anne

Dancing Bear bosses are among the easiest to manage. They're predictable. They're pleasers. They get the lay of the upward political land. Use them to your advantage. Increase your ability to get your job done by aligning your strategy with theirs. Everyone will win.

Chapter 3
KING OF THE MOUNTAIN

By Bryant

What leaders DO, what companies DO, is way more important than what they say. Listen to the talk they walk.

Chapter 4
A DOSE OF REALITY

By Bryant

Hold your leaders accountable, help them improve by giving them your honest feedback, and have the moral courage to call out their inadequacies.

Chapter 5
THE QUEEN OF DENIAL

By Bryant

There's a ton of material available to improve your leadership ability. Take charge, step up, and go after it. If your boss needs help in this area and won't seek it out, maybe a few anonymous educational gifts should be considered.

Chapter 6
EYE OF THE BEHOLDER

By Anne

Identify your boss' weaknesses and play smarter. Take on the mindset that the whole is greater than the sum of it parts. Realize that your boss has weaknesses, set yourself up to compliment those weaknesses, and set yourselves up to be a stronger team.

Chapter 7
TICK TOCK

By Bryant

Make a decision already! Do we need to put a gun to your head? What will it take for you to make up your mind and let your people off the hook? Please remember what it was like for you to be in that position. Instead of being a boss that sucks, if there's something you can do to make the process faster, more efficient, easier for your people and your company, please do it TODAY.

Chapter 8
KNOW WHEN TO FOLD 'EM

By Anne

Someone may have promised you a rose garden, but roses don't smell like that. Know when to get out! Believe in yourself enough to know that you deserve a future filled with possibility. Find that future!

Chapter 9
OOPS!

By Bryant

No matter how skilled we are at performing our jobs, there is always potential to learn something new about ourselves or look at an issue from another viewpoint. Mistakes are generally lessons in disguise, and are designed to prevent us from making a larger mistake in the future. Cherish your mistakes because they represent growth, and always, ALWAYS, check your target.

Chapter 10
CLOUD SNEEZES

By Anne

Surprise yourself today. Do something, say something, be something that you've wanted to do, say, or be. Find one brave thing and do it! And find one thing in someone else. Let it be that surprising thing that you search for in those you know so well.

Chapter 11
IT TAKES TACT

By Anne

Embrace your weaknesses, understand them, and then work on your strengths. Our strengths are the areas in which we can gain the greatest ground. We would never ask a gifted cellist to learn how to play the guitar in order to be a great musician. We would ask the cellist to continue to practice the cello. The same applies to you and your gifts.

Chapter 12
MAKING IT STICK

By Anne

Just try to keep your subconscious from making a point! If your mouth isn't saying it, some other part of your body is. We communicate to people in a myriad of different ways, and people communicate to us in even more. Pay attention to what you're "saying." And it's important to "note" that every now and again a really good boss comes along. You and a good boss can create a magical relationship, and some powerful business results. Hold a high bar for good bosses, and help make them better. Get yourself some really small Post-it® notes to carry the message, and see what happens.

Chapter 13
PLAN B

By Bryant

You're not stuff, so don't let yourself be treated that way. You're a valuable asset to the organization. Work for one that treats you that way.

Chapter 14
FALL OUT

By Bryant

Follow your heart. You know the best thing to do for you. Do that and it will be the best thing you can do for others. Be the leader you were meant to be.

Chapter 15
GOAT RODEO

By Anne

Find work that stretches you, that takes you out of your comfort zone enough that you can grow. Find it in a place that you want to be, doing things you want to be doing, with people you want to be doing it with. Never saddle up for less than your best ride.

Chapter 16
COWBOY UP!

By Anne

Cowboy up! Do everything you can to help your boss become a better boss. Cowboy up also means that you do what it takes for your own personal development. It means you seek feedback, learn from experiences, and persist in getting the job done well. Here's our question for you: have you done all YOU can do? If the answer is no, then get moving. It's time for you to cowboy up!

Chapter 17
COW ENERGY

By Anne

It's your energy and it can't be blocked unless you let it. Make sure you always have a clear path forward, and clear the way for others while you're at it.

Chapter 18
THE UNREASONABLE MAN

By Bryant

Be brave enough to put it out there, have the courage to be unreasonable, and be smart about it. Tremendous results can be obtained through shock and awe.

Chapter 19
NOW WHAT?

By Anne

You ALWAYS have the power to choose. Not choosing is a choice. Your circumstance is your circumstance because you have chosen it. Choose an outcome that you can be happy with. Live well!

Everybody currently has, has had, or will have a boss that sucks!

Share your bad boss experience with us for possible inclusion in our next book:
MY BOSS SUCKS TOO

Submit your stories online at **www.bossfixers.com** or mail them to:

HALSTEAD Attn: My Boss Sucks Too P.O. Box 6153 Fredericksburg, VA 22403	Your submission must include the following: Full name* Address Phone Number Email (if applicable)

*Only your first name and the first letter of your last name (or alias if requested) will be published if your story is used for the book.

The submission of your story via email or hard copy constitutes permission for its use as is or in part with any necessary modifications deemed appropriate by HALSTEAD. You will be notified if your story will be published and no promise of compensation is expressed or implied by HALSTEAD.

If you need further information or have questions about your submission, feel free to contact HALSTEAD at: 540.735.4944

HOW DO YOU GET MORE COPIES
OF MY BOSS SUCKS?

Order online at **www.bossfixers.com**

Or

Contact us with order requests using the info below.

Quantity Discounts Available - For More Info Call: 540.735.4944

HALSTEAD

P.O. Box 6153

Fredericksburg, VA 22403

Phone - 540.735.4944

Fax - 540.752.0871